Federico García Lorca (1898–1936) is Europe's most beloved poet and playwright. His poems and plays about creation, desire and death have been translated into dozens of languages and transformed into song, ballet, opera, film, and painting. Fascinated by the folk music of his native Spain, Lorca wrote two books inspired by gypsy rhythms: *Poem of the Deep Song* (on the world of flamenco and cante jondo) and the best-selling *Gypsy Ballads*. In *Poet in New York* (written 1929–1930) he turns the American city into an image of universal loneliness, and in tragedies like *Yerma*, *Blood Wedding*, and *The House of Bernarda Alba* he takes the measure of human longing and of the social repression that would contribute to his early death (he was shot by right-wing forces at the beginning of the Spanish Civil War). In the *Gypsy Ballads*, translated by Jane Duran and Gloria García Lorca and published by Enitharmon Press in 2011, the poet transforms into metaphor and myth the fantasy and reality of a marginalized people.

In *The Tamarit Divan* and the *Sonnets of Dark Love*, written toward the end of Lorca's brief life, desire and death come together in poetic chiaroscuro. In these dark and final meditations and flashes of passion, the poet pays homage to Spanish mystics, to Italian masters of the sonnet, and to the Arab poets of his native Andalusia.

Translated and introduced by Jane Duran and Gloria García Lorca

with essays by
Christopher Maurer
Andrés Soria Olmedo

ENITHARMON PRESS

Federico García Lorca

Sonnets of Dark Love

The Tamarit Divan

for Isabel García Lorca de los Rios
and Laura García Lorca de los Rios

Diván del Tamarit

Gacelas

Casidas

The Tamarit Divan

Ghazals

Qasidas

Sonetos del amor oscuro

Sonnets of Dark Love

Acknowledgements

Christopher Maurer has been an invaluable critic and support while we were working on these translations. We thank him warmly for his insights, advice and enthusiasm, and for translating the essay by Andrés Soria Olmedo.

We are immensely grateful to Andrés Soria Olmedo for his clarity in response to our questions and doubts raised by the text. Our warm thanks to Cheli Durán and Mimi Khalvati for their thoughtful reading of these translations and their perceptive comments and suggestions.

The Spanish text for both books is from the Collected Poems edited by Christopher Maurer (New York: Farrar, Straus and Giroux, 2002), and we have drawn on his detailed notes to the text and poems. Two other editions also include valuable textual notes and commentary: Diván del Tamarit, Llanto por Ignacio Sánchez Mejías, Sonetos edited by Mario Hernández (Madrid: Alianza Editorial, 1989); and Miguel García-Posada's edition of Obras Completas I, (Barcelona: Círculo de Lectores/Galaxia Gutenberg, 1996). Lorca's Late Poetry: A Critical Study by Andrew A. Anderson (Leeds: Francis Cairns Ltd, 1990) offers a detailed, penetrating analysis of the poems and their literary context and references. The fascinating, informative Poemas arabigoandaluces translated and edited by Emilio García Gómez (Madrid: Espasa-Calpe, 1959) opens a window on the poetry of Arab Andalusia.

Our thanks to John Morgan and Teresa Lima for their dedication to this project, and for creating another beautiful book that reflects with sensitivity the language and tone of Lorca's poetry.

We are very grateful to Isabel Brittain at Enitharmon Press for her support in promoting this book. Our warm thanks as ever to our editor, Stephen Stuart-Smith, for his generous commitment to this project, his faith in our work as translators, and his fine editing of this book.

Preface

Jane Duran & Gloria García Lorca

As love poems of his maturity, The Tamarit Divan and the Sonnets
of Dark Love are less widely known and celebrated than other works
by Lorca such as the Gypsy Ballads, Poet in New York or his Lament
for Ignacio Sanchez Mejías. We thought it would be illuminating to
publish an edition in which the two books could lie side by side
and be compared as explorations of passionate love.

These collections were published posthumously. Lorca wrote
the 21 poems in the Diván del Tamarit between 1931 and 1934. The
eleven poems gathered later under the title Sonetos del amor oscuro
were written between 1935 and 1936. Ten of these poems were early
drafts, written on hotel notepaper, his first collection of love poems
addressed to a specific, but unnamed person.

This book follows on our translations of Lorca's Gypsy Ballads
(2011), in which there is an Andalusian flavour to the language,
imagery and narratives, in a defined physical landscape. There the
protagonists are gypsies and natural forces, but in the Diván and
the Sonetos we hear only the solitary voice of the poet. Both the Sonnets
of Dark Love and The Tamarit Divan take us to the border of the poet's
pain where what is felt is almost unbearable. Although an intensity
of pain and vulnerability is characteristic of Lorca's poetry, in these
last two books this quality is heightened.

> Between gypsum and jasmine, your gaze
> was a pale branch of seeds.
> I searched my breast to give you
> the ivory letters that say *always*.
>
> *Always, always*: garden of my agony,
> your body forever fugitive,
> the blood of your veins in my mouth,
> your mouth with no light for my death.
>
> ['Of unforeseen love']

The Tamarit Divan explores many facets of love, but the 'you', the beloved, remains elusive: a 'garden of my agony'. Most of the poems were already written and many published, some with different titles, when Lorca collected them, bringing a unifying Arabic flavour to the collection. He was familiar with and admired the Persian and Arabic poets, the 'maravilloso Omar Khayyam' and the 'sublimes gacelas amorosas de Hafiz'. He had read Emilio García Gómez's translations of Arab-Andalusian poetry. According to Francisco García Lorca, the poet's brother, this was the only book Lorca decided to write before he had actually composed any of the poems.

The poems in the Divan are divided into *ghazals* and *qasidas*. The classic *qasida* is a long, monorhymed, metred poem in couplets. Traditionally it began with the evocation of and lament for a lost beloved (the *nasid*). Other elements could include a solitary journey through the desert, and a final panegyric or satire. The *ghazal* evolved from the opening section of the *qasida*, the *nasid*, and is a short monorhymed poem in metre and self-contained couplets, with a refrain repeated at the end of each couplet. It is associated with song and speaks of human or mystical love, separation and longing.

Yet while Lorca's poems may carry echoes of those Arabic and Persian forms, they are varied in their metre, rhyme schemes and line lengths. His poems draw on Spanish metrical forms and some recall traditional or popular songs:

> Only to hear
> the bell of the Vela
> I crowned you with verbena.
>
> *Granada was a moon*
> *drowned in ivy.*
>
> Only to hear
> the bell of the Vela
> I tore out my garden of Cartagena.
>
> *Granada was a pink doe*
> *among the weathervanes.*

Only to hear
the bell of the Vela
I burned in your body
not knowing whose it was.

['Of the love that hides itself']

Although the mystical dimension so intrinsic to Arab and
Persian poetry and its symbolism is absent in Lorca's *Divan*, what
the love poems do share with this poetry is a heightened, ecstatic
tone and sensuality, praise of the beloved and a sense of unfulfilled
love. The references to the Arab-Andalusian culture Lorca so
loved, the 'admirable civilisation' whose loss he lamented, brings
an additional dimension or resonance to love poems infused
with longing and the sense that love is unattainable and
inseparable from death.

Granada is a city marked by its Moorish past, a city that sits
beneath the Sierra Nevada's white gaze, and whose thirst is
quenched by the two rivers that irrigate Granada's Vega or fertile
plain, the river Darro and the Genil. The irrigation systems are
part of this Moorish past and they bring water to the farmlands
as well as to the city and its gardens.

I want to go down to the well,
I want to climb the walls of Granada
to see the heart pierced
by the dark awl of the waters.

[QASIDA I: 'Of the one wounded by water']

Granada's gardens are one of the many examples of this Moorish heritage. They are exquisite enclosures, intimate and refined. Lorca wrote many of the poems in the *Divan* at his cousin's *huerta* or farm that, following the Moorish tradition, included a garden with quince trees and pomegranates, roses and jasmine. A spiral and a straight line, the shapes of Arab calligraphy, the rigid column topped by the softness of the Arab arch, the blinding southern sunlight and the coolness of the patio: his is a heritage of cultural and aesthetic contrasts, and these are reflected in his work, creating poetic tension and metaphors for his emotional struggle.

> Jasmine flower and wounded bull.
> Infinite pavement. Map. Room. Harp. Dawn.
> The girl dreams of a jasmine bull
> and the bull is a bloody sunset that roars.
>
> [QASIDA V: 'Of the dream in open air']

In an interview in 1936, Lorca spoke of a book called *Sonetos* that he was planning to publish: 'The book of *Sonnets* signifies a return to traditional form after a spacious and sunny walk through the freedom of metre and rhyme.' In the *Sonnets of Dark Love* Lorca leaves the garden behind and enters a space that is darker, exposed and intimate. Here there is an intuition of approaching ends. The exquisite *Divan* verses have given way to a poetry formally contained, that both protects and permits the poet to speak without filters. They explore a single relationship, laying bare the poet's feelings and sexual orientation.

> This light, this fire that devours,
> this grey landscape that surrounds me,
> this pain that comes from one idea only,
> this anguish of sky, world and hour
>
> ['Wounds of love']

Whereas the *Divan* is a combination of different poetic forms and rhyme schemes, evoking the variety of plants and trees in a garden, everything is order, symmetry and steady rhythm in the *Sonnets of Dark Love*. The Petrarchan sonnet becomes a structure for Lorca's passionate and desperate verses of unusual power and modernity. We wonder what changes and polish he might have added to a finished manuscript, yet these early drafts have a raw energy. Directed to only one person, they are intimate confessions of his struggle with love and sexual longing. Within the constraints of the sonnet form, he sustains an intense emotional climate as well as a sense of urgency, a need to speak openly about the turmoil and pain of love lost.

As in our translation of the *Gypsy Ballads*, our aim has been to stay as close as possible to Lorca's tone and meanings. Occasionally we have had to modify a phrase, but as a rule we have remained faithful to the original text and the integrity of his images. In so doing, although we cannot transpose his intricate and subtle sound patterns, we have tried to convey the singularity of the poet's voice with all its conflicting emotions.

> And the sun entered the closed balcony
> and the coral of life opened its branch
> over my shrouded heart.

Violet Shadow

Christopher Maurer

The title – *Diván del Tamarit* – alludes to a place outside Granada that
García Lorca loved: the Huerta del Tamarit, country home of a paternal
uncle and of his favourite cousin. As at his family's own home, the
Huerta de San Vicente, a short walk away, the poet would have been
vividly aware that, centuries earlier, the lands had been farmed
and ingeniously watered, by Muslims who had been expelled from
Spain in 1492. It was at the Huerta del Tamarit, with its view of the
snowcapped Sierra and the poplar groves of the Vega, that some of
the poems were written, between 1931 and 1934. They were gathered
into a *divan* – Persian word for a collection of poems by a single author
– in the autumn of 1934 and were to have been published by the
University of Granada, as Lorca's personal 'homage to the old Arab
poets of Granada.'[1] The book was well into production – proofs had
already been pulled – but the start of the Spanish Civil War brought
an end to the project.[2] In one of his last public interviews – June 1936,
two months before his assassination in Granada – the poet offers
some scathing words about the expulsion of the Moors. 'It was an
evil moment, despite what they teach us at school. An admirable
civilization was lost, a poetry, an astronomy, an architecture and
a refinement unique in all the world, to make way for a poor, cowardly
city, a two-bit city where, presently, one finds the worst bourgeoisie
in all Spain.'[3] In Granada such statements did not go unpunished.
It was not until 1940 that Lorca's *Diván* was published, and not in
Granada but in New York, where his family was living in exile.[4] It
would be another 14 years before a complete edition appeared in Spain.

The *Diván* is Lorca's most beautiful and haunting book of poems.[5]
It is also his most sombre, as though written in the shadow of death.
Lorca describes the Tamarit as the 'jardín de mi *agonía*', the garden
where, amid the play of water, he battles death.[6] He composed his
Divan around the same time as he was working out his theory of artistic

creation in the lecture 'Play and Theory of the Duende' (1933),
one of whose lessons is that great art – music, painting, poetry –
requires an acute awareness of death:

> The duende doesn't come at all unless he sees that death
> is possible. The duende must know beforehand that death
> will serenade his house and can rock the branches we
> all wear, branches that do not have, will never have, any
> consolation [7]

Those mortal branches are at their breaking point in the Tamarit
poems:

> In the groves of Tamarit
> there are many children with veiled faces
> waiting for my branches to fall,
> waiting for them to break on their own.

The poet is alone in his Gethsemane, tensing his desire against
death, speaking his final will and testament, searching for
a 'light-filled death' to consume him, far from the dark jumble
of cemeteries (GHAZAL X, 'Of the flight', GHAZAL VIII, 'Of the dark
death'). [8] In Lorca's Lament for Ignacio Sánchez Mejías, a child brings
a white shroud; here, on the night of his passing, a mysteriously
'wounded hand' will bring the oils of extreme unction and the
'white sheet of my agony' (QASIDA VI). The presence of children
– the 'children with veiled faces' in the house and garden and
orchard of this death-conscious poet – makes the poems pulse with
urgency and desire: 'I want...', 'Yo quiero que...', 'No quiero que...'

> I want the water to have no riverbed.
> I want the wind to have no valleys.
>
> I want the night to lose its eyes
> and my heart its flower of gold...
>
> [GHAZAL II]

Everywhere the poet looks, desire and longing are defeated by death or – like the rose – 'immobile in the sky' (QASIDA VII). 'There is hardly a poem in the book, no matter how sharp or graceful,' writes Lorca's friend Angel del Río, who co-ordinated the New York edition of *Diván*, 'where there is not death, blood, or weeping.'[9]

The anxiously imagined death occurs in a poetic space familiar to the poet: an orchard or garden (the poems refer to an *arboleda*, a *jardín*, a *huerto*). Any Spanish poet writing at the beginning of the twentieth century could versify ad infinitum about 'Romantic' encounters in moonlit gardens, but Lorca had his own keen sense of their pathos, especially in Granada, a city he associated with different forms of enclosure: the *carmen* (house with walled garden, the image of paradise loved by the Arabs); the convent garden; the filthy fenced-in gardens of railway stations; the abandoned gardens of autumn (faded roses, nightingales); the 'Gardens Open to Few' of the Baroque poet Pedro Soto de Rojas, where the book itself takes the form of a garden.[10] Closer still to the world of the Tamarit is the imaginary space, haunted by sex, childhood, and death, of 'Double Poem of Lake Eden', in *Poet in New York*.[11]

•

One of Lorca's friends snapped a photo of him, around 1924, in improvised turban and Moorish robe. The occasion has been forgotten, but the playful pose is a reminder of the possibilities and pitfalls of the Spanish orientalism that formed part of his Andalusian *milieu* and to which he himself was sometimes subjected: a distinguished English critic, visiting Granada in the early 1920s, one of the first foreigners to notice his work, wrote about Lorca as 'a poet of Arabia' and many others have done so over the years. Visible from the terrace of his family's home at the Huerta de San Vicente, where he wrote some of the *Diván*, was the Alhambra, 'aesthetic axis of the city, miniature palace that Andalusian fantasy saw through the wrong end of its binoculars'.[12] That privileged vista – the Alhambra against the backdrop of the Sierra Nevada – must have posed a poetic challenge. The 'mysterious oriental venom' that suffuses literature about the East – whether the Far East or the local Andalusian East – could be fatal to poetry, and the Alhambra, with its fragile beauty and metaphorical status as *divan* (some of the qasidas of Ibn Zamrak were 'published' on its walls [13]) had become the epicentre of sentimentalizing verse and Orientalist kitsch. In his own work Lorca pushes away the nostalgic props of Hispanic *modernismo*: the 'sleepy odalisques' and silent emirs, sultry sultanas, fountains that sing like guzlas, scimitars and soft-eyed gazelles.[14] An early poem like 'Canción. Ensueño y confusión' (Song: Reverie and Confusion), written in 1917, stands out as an exception. Here is what Lorca would spend his life *avoiding*, except in parody and jest:

> Fue una noche plena de lujuria
> Noche de oro en Oriente ancestral
> Noche de besos, de luz y caricias
> Noche encarnada de tul pasional.

> It was a night filled with lust,
> A golden night in the ancestral Orient,
> A night of kisses, of light and caresses
> A flesh-toned night of impassioned tulle.[15]

At an early age Lorca learned to elude all that: the golden stars pinned to the oddly impassioned tulle. His *Diván del Tamarit* arose, rather, from an enduring feeling of admiration and poetic kinship. Just a few years after he began writing verse, he had begun to think that the traditional poetry of Andalusia – the fatalistic *deep song* lyrics or *coplas* that, in 1921–1922, seemed to him the most intense of all Spanish poems – bore special affinity with Eastern verse:

> When our songs reach the very extremes of pain and love
> they become sisters in expression to the magnificent verses
> of Arabian and Persian poets.

The truth is that in the air of Córdoba and Granada one still finds gestures and lines of remote Arabia, and that remembrances of lost cities still arise from the murky palimpsest of the Albaicín.

The same themes of sacrifice, undying love, and wine, expressed in the same spirit, appear [both in deep song lyrics and] in the works of mysterious Asiatic poets.[16]

Lorca's basis for those statements, and the source of his examples, from Hafez and from 'mysterious' Arabic poets, was an early nineteenth-century compilation of Asiatic Poems (Poesías asiáticas): translations from English and Latin versions of Persian and Arabic verse, edited by Gaspar María de Nava (1760–1815). Another source of inspiration would have been Goethe's tribute to Hafez, his West-östlicher Divan. The idea of tradition, and of the palimpsest, would endure in Lorca's work: [17] an image of the Andalusian character as an overlay of civilizations – Tartesian, Roman, Christian, Gypsy, Jewish, Arab – sometimes with agonistic overtones. Architecture and character were bound closely together:

The prodigious mass of the Cathedral [of Granada] the great imperial and Roman stamp of Carlos V, exist alongside the little store of the Jew who prays before an image beaten from the silver of the menorah, just as the tombs of the Catholic Monarchs [in the Cathedral] have not kept the half-moon from coming out at times on the chests of Granada's finest sons. The struggle goes obscurely, without expressing itself; well, not exactly without expression, for on the city's Colina Roja, its red hill, are two dead palaces – the Alhambra and the Palace of Charles V – that duel to the death in the consciousness of every present-day inhabitant of Granada.

Whatever the undercurrent of conflict – that 'duel to the death' – Granada's mixed heritage was to be cherished. Months after Lorca's remarks about *cante jondo* lyrics, in summer 1922 – while Spain was fighting entirely real, not imagined Berbers in northern Africa – the poet was plotting with friends to build a 'marabout' – a Muslim shrine or hermitage – on a donated plot of land on the outskirts of Granada. The monument (he remarks in a letter) would honour

> Ibn Tufail and two or three other geniuses of Arab culture in Granada. Inside, we would create a library of Granadan/Arabic things and outside, around the monument, we would plant willows, palms, and cypresses. What joy it would be... to see from Puerta Real [a square in Granada] the white cupola of the marabout and its little tower keeping it company. Also, this would be the first memory devoted in Spain to these sublime Granadans of the purest stock, who loom large in the world of Islam.... We are also thinking of inviting learned Moors from all over the East, who would come to Granada, and of making an anthology of Ibn Tufail, edited by [José] Navarro [Pardo], with things that I myself would contribute for the occasion. We hope the cupola of the shrine will be starred, like that of the Arab baths, and Manolo Ortiz will decorate the interior with hieratic, suggestive oriental themes? What do you think? [18]

The idea of a monument honouring the twelfth-century writer and philosopher and other 'wise men' never came to fruition, but a decade later Lorca's professor and mentor Fernando de los Ríos, then Minister of Education (with whom Lorca seems to have travelled to Morocco) signed into existence schools of Arabic Studies in Madrid and Granada. The latter was placed under the direction of Emilio García Gómez, whose anthology of *Arab-Andalusian Poems* (1930) – a major effort of translation from the original Arabic – was an inspiration for Lorca's *Diván*, as it was for other poets of his generation. [19]

One of them, Luis Cernuda, spoke of 'themes, styles, common concerns' that remove Lorca's *Diván* from a narrow, Spanish context and link it with 'eastern' poetry.[20] García Gómez himself points to affinities: the city personified as the beloved (GHAZAL IV); the theme of the nocturnal tryst (GHAZAL III); an amorous tone that 'vaguely recalls the morbid pseudo-chastity of the Bedouin' (GHAZAL II); and what he calls the 'daring excess' of some metaphors (rivalling that of Luis de Góngora). More recent scholars have noted other similarities, from the frequent mention of plants and fruits to the agonizing separation of the lovers: the ghazal as elegy. Edwin Honig, one of the *Diván*'s first translators, writes that, 'like the best Arabic issue,' these poems celebrate 'the esthetic of sensual form in fleeting time.'[21]

But Lorca seldom takes his cues directly from medieval Arabic poetry. His voice is never more entirely his own than in this evocation of the Andalusian *other*. The nineteenth century, he once said, had 'masked' his city in a 'perverse bland of Orientalism.' But nineteenth-century Romanticism had its aesthetic uses. When he writes about Andalusia, Lorca sometimes does so with an approving nod to French and American visitors to his city – Théophile Gautier, Washington Irving, Victor Hugo – not because he wants to imitate those authors but because they set him free from an oppressively 'local' tradition and help him avoid the poetic dead-ends of Andalusian nationalism. 'Arab Andalusia' was a potent symbol on either side of the Strait. While steering clear of that sort of patriotic nostalgia, Lorca wanted to suggest, to allude, to evoke, to stylize – to write 'in the manner of' another aesthetic moment. As Andrés Soria Olmedo puts it, in the *Diván*, Lorca creates 'a space of metaphysical Romanticism that is uniquely his own.'[22]

What Lorca did find in classical Arabic poetry that he could not have found in the Spanish poets who preceded him were cultural precedents for the homoeroticism of his ghazals[23] (in his usage, 'ghazal' seems generally to mean 'love poem'). In those where the beloved is mentioned, grammatical gender is eluded, as it is in the *Sonnets*, but the imagery suggests masculinity or homoerotic love: 'pale branch of seeds' (I), 'your clean nakedness, / like a black cactus open in the reeds' (II),

'reed of love, wet jasmine' (IX).[24] Whether the Diván pays homage
to the sublimated erotic suffering of Udhrah love, as García
Gómez seems to suggest, is not easy to say. The desire of the Diván
is all encompassing, as is the image of death, which transcends
that of the poet and colours everything around him: yellows invade
the silks, time flows painfully under broken arches, the dead are
weeping under the bed ...

> The rest all passes.
> A blush with no name. Perpetual star.
> The rest is the other: sad wind,
> while the leaves rush away in flocks.

Diván del Tamarit leaves us with the consolation of poetry – the
mystery, the violet shadow of the poet's hands and voice, speaking
calmly, despite the dark.

1 In a 'Note' published with the *Diván* (and reprinted in the editions by Mario Hernández and by Andrew A. Anderson) the scholar Emilio García Gómez remembers telling the poet that he wanted to dedicate a book to Ibn Zamrak, 'whose poems have been published in the most de luxe edition the world has ever seen: the Alhambra itself, where they cover the walls, adorn the rooms, and circle the basins of fountains. Lorca then told us that he had composed, in homage to these old Granadan poets, a collection of casidas and ghazals, that is, a *Divan*... Antonio Gallego Burín, as dean of the School of Letters, asked him for the manuscript. Pleased, Lorca gave his consent. Francisco Prieto offered to design the cover. I made the commitment – may the reader forgive me – to write these lines.' (Anderson, p. 184)

2 For a detailed chronology of composition, revision and publication, see the critical edition of Andrew A. Anderson, *Diván del Tamarit, Seis poemas galegos, Llanto por Ignacio Sánchez Mejías* (Madrid: Espasa-Calpe, 1988), 24–31 and 53–112, and for the best possible introduction, with comments on the hermeticism of *Diván* and on Lorca's debt to traditional Spanish song, Mario Hernández, ed., *Diván del Tamarit, Llanto por Ignacio Sánchez Mejías, Sonetos* (Madrid: Alianza Editorial, 1981).

3 'Conversation with Bagaría' (*El Sol*, 10 June 1936), Christopher Maurer, ed., *Deep Song and Other Prose* (New York: New Directions, 1980), p. 130. Bagaría had asked, 'Do you think it was entirely right to return the keys of your native Granada?'

4 It was published in the same city and year as *Poet in New York*.

5 Mario Hernández (10), for example, considers it 'one of the most complex and polished' of Lorca's works, and 'one of the great books of European poetry'.

6 The *Diccionario de la Lengua Española* defines *agonía* as 'the anguish and distress of one dying; the state preceding death.'

7. *In Search of Duende*, ed. Christopher Maurer (New York: New Directions, 1998), p. 58.

8 Like the cicada, in Lorca's early poem of that title: 'Cicada, you are fortunate / to die on a bed of light.'

9 Angel del Río, *Estudios sobre literatura contemporánea española* (Madrid: Gredos, 1966), p. 247.

10 See the lecture on Soto de Rojas, 'Paraíso cerrado para muchos, jardines abiertos para pocos...' ('Paradise Closed to Many, Gardens Open to Few') in *Obras completas*, Vol. III, *Prosa*, ed. Miguel García-Posada (Barcelona: Galaxia Gutenberg/Círculo de Lectores, 1997), pp. 78–87.

11 For Lorca's remarks on gardens, see the beginning of *Impressions and Landscapes*, tr. Lawrence Klibbe (University Press of America, 1987), pp. 95 ff.

12 *Obras completas*, III, p. 8.

13 James T. Monroe, *Hispano-Arabic Poetry; A Student Anthology* (Berkeley/Los Angeles/London: University of California Press), 1974, p. 65.

14 For a great repository of these clichés and others – an arsenal of Andalusian Orientalism – see the poetry of Francisco Villaespesa, the première of whose play, *El alcázar de las perlas*, Lorca may have seen in Granada in 1911; cf. Francisco García Lorca, *In the Green Morning: Memories of Federico* (New York: New Directions), p. 56. The poet and playwright José de Zorrilla would have been another much celebrated source of Orientalist imagery. Lorca went so far as to mock that Orientalist tradition in a poem – 'Granada as Sultan' – by an apocryphal poet of his own invention. See *Antología modelna*, ed. Miguel García-Posada (Granada: La Veleta, 1995), p. 39.

15 *Poesía inédita de juventud*, ed. Christian de Paepe (Madrid: Cátedra, 1994), p. 25.

16 *Deep Song*, pp. 36–37.

17 See, for example, 'Palimpsests', in *Collected Poems*, ed. Christopher Maurer (New York: Farrar, Straus and Giroux, 4th ed., 2013), pp. 212–219. As Eric Calderwood observes, the Romantics invented an Al-Andalus 'predicated on the discovery of a palimpsestic past that lurks just below the surface of the present – indeed, a past that, at times, bleeds into and overwhelms the present.' See 'The Invention of Al-Andalus: Discovering the Past and Creating the Present in Granada's Islamic Tourism Sites', *The Journal of North African Studies* 19.1 (2014), pp. 27–55.

18 Letter to Melchor Fernández Almagro, 1 July 1922, in *Epistolario completo*, ed. Andrew A. Anderson and Christopher Maurer (Madrid: Cátedra, 1997), 148–49. On this project, mentioned again in 1928, and on related ones, see Nicolás Antonio Fernández's rich and detailed study of Lorca and Granada in the 1920s and 1930s, *Federico García Lorca y el grupo de la revista* gallo (Granada: Diputación de Granada, 2012), pp. 58–60.

19 Editorial Plutarco, 1930, with some of the poems pre-published in *Revista de Occidente* (Madrid), 1928. There is an English translation, based on García Gómez's Spanish, by Cola Franzen, *Poems of Arab Andalusia* (San Francisco: City Lights Books, 1989). García Gómez's prologue ('Nota') for Lorca's *Diván* was not published together with the poems until Mario Hernández's edition of 1981.

20 Alberti is quoted in Cola Franzen, p. ii. Cernuda considered the *Diván* less 'orientalist' than other works by Lorca, 'despite his somewhat arbitrary use of the terms "casida" and "ghazal".' 'Federico García Lorca (1898–1936)', *Obras completas*, vol. II, *Prosa*, ed. Derek Harris and Luis Maristany (Madrid: Siruela, 1994), p. 212.

21 *García Lorca* (New York: New Directions, 1963), p. 93. For a discussion of similarities between the *Diván* and Arabic poetry, C. B. Morris, *Son of Andalusia. The Lyrical Landscapes of Federico García Lorca* (Nashville: Vanderbilt University Press, 1997), pp. 399–407; M. Ángeles Pérez Álvarez, 'La influencia oriental en el *Diván del Tamarit* de Lorca', *Anuario de Estudios Filológicos* 15 (1992), pp. 69–78. Evelyn Scaramella thoughtfully explores the 'subversive' ideological and historical implications of Lorca's Moorish imagery in 'Past and Present Politics: Visions of the *romances fronterizos* in Lorca's *Romancero gitano*', *Journal of the Midwest Modern Language Association* 42:2 (2009), pp. 137–158. It is worth remembering that Lorca once proposed to García Gómez that they also edit a book of Morisco ballads ('Lorca y su Diván del Tamarit', *ABC* [Madrid], 5 February 1982, p. 3).

22 Federico García Lorca, *Sólo un caballo azul y una madrugada. Antología poética (1917–1935)*, ed. Andrés Soria Olmedo (Barcelona: Galaxia Gutenberg/Círculo de Lectores, 2004), p. 27.

23 What he understood by 'qasida' is less precise. In an introductory note to the *Diván*, García Gómez explains: 'in Arabic casida is the name given to every poem of a certain length, with a certain internal architecture (the detail is unimportant here), in verses with a single rhyme, measured according to scrupulously conventional patterns' (ed. Anderson, p.184). It seems 'obvious' to him that Lorca's use of both terms – ghazal and qasida – was 'in a sense, arbitrary.' Lorca would also have been aware of the term's use both in the music of Northern Africa and other Arabic regions, and in modernist composers like Conrado del Campo, in 'Una Kasida. Poema en cuatro momentos' (ca. 1920). The word was used indiscriminately in the popular press to evoke 'the fragrant poetic soul of Andalusia', and other chimeras.

24 On precedents, see Jerry W. Wright and Everett K. Rowson, *Homoeroticism in Classical Arabic Literature* (New York: Columbia University, 1997) and Khaled El-Rouayheb, *Before Homosexuality in the Arab-Islamic World, 1500–1800* (Chicago: University of Chicago Press, 2005).

Dark St Valentine

Andrés Soria Olmedo

Between 1935 and 1936 Lorca wrote eleven love sonnets that form
a well-defined cycle, broken off by his murder in 1936. When he
wrote these sonnets he was following a certain tendency of the
1930s, popular among the youngest poets: the return to metre and
to the stanza as a sign of poetic *maestría* – a tendency simultaneous,
and not incompatible, with free verse and its rhetoric. Lorca's eleven
sonnets were published together for the first time in a pirated
edition in December 1983, followed by an 'authorized edition' in
ABC, the Madrid daily newspaper, in 1984, and then become part of
his canon. The poet spoke of preparing a book of *Sonnets*, and in 1936,
of a *Garden of Sonnets*. But the most memorable title has been *Sonnets
of Dark Love*, mentioned in 1937 by his friend Vicente Aleixandre, for
whom the poems were 'a prodigy of passion, of enthusiasm, of joy,
of torment, a pure and ardent monument to love.' Other great poets
– Luis Cernuda, Pablo Neruda – followed him in their praise and
in their mention of that title.

Lorca himself spoke in 1927 of the *amores oscuros* (dark loves) of
the Baroque poet the Count of Villamediana, and used the phrase
in one of the sonnets: 'Oh secret voice of dark love!' According
to Aleixandre, 'his love was one of difficult passion, battered and
bruised, dark and painful, unrequited or badly lived... dark because
of the sinister destiny of love without destiny, without future.'
Mario Hernández writes that dark love is 'inevitably associated
with death', while for José Angel Valente, the dark is tied specifically
to a 'primitive form of death' – the 'impossibility of engendering
children', and the 'non-germinative character of the homosexual
relationship', as in the sonnet 'Adam', signed in New York on
1 December 1929, a prelude to the cycle: 'Adam dreams in the fever
of the clay / a child who comes galloping / in the double pulse of
his cheek. // But another dark Adam is dreaming / a neutral moon

of seedless stone / where the child of light will be burnt'. For
Andrew Anderson, *oscuro* means Dionysiacal and tragic, as well
as secret, intimate, and hidden from public view.

The adjective *oscuro* and its connotations appear in other works.
In *The Audience* the White Horse wishes to carry Juliet off 'into
the dark.' 'And what will you give me there?' she asks trembling.
'I will give you what is most hushed in the dark.' In *Diván del Tamarit*,
'No one understood the perfume / of the dark magnolia of your
belly' (GHAZAL I, 'Of unforeseen love'). And in the final scene
of *Blood Wedding* the Bride admits: 'Your son was a little bit of water
from which I hoped for children, land, health; but the other man
was a dark river, full of brush that pulled me close to the murmur
and humming of its reeds.'

The confessional mode is in the very character of the love sonnet
as poetic form, for, as Lorca wrote in 1924, 'the sonnet preserves
an eternal feeling that fits into no poetic vessel but this apparently
cold one.' The amorous confession also arises from the ample
conventions of Petrarchism, a poetic language codified in the
sixteenth century in Spain and spoken throughout Europe, a sort
of poetic esperanto that served as channel for a poetic river born
among Greeks and Latins – a river which pooled up in Provence
and in the Italians of the *dolce stil nuovo*, and in Petrarch, and again
at the beginning of the sixteenth century when Bembo thought
it a classical form worthy of imitation and propagated it through
printing, and again in the seventeenth, when the unity of the
sonnet cycle or *canzoniere* fractured into a thousand themes and
motifs. The Hispanic dialect of that Petrarchan language is that
of Garcilaso, Herrera, Góngora, Lope, Quevedo, Soto de Rojas...

At every stage of the journey, poetic forms and doctrines are
superimposed on one another. From the Ancients comes writing
'in praise of some female friend ... Virgil wrote about Lidia, whom
he greatly loved. Ovid... about Corinna, Catullus, about Lesbia;
Propertius, Cynthia; Tibullus, Flavia... Dante, about Beatrice, and
Miser Francesco about Madonna Laura' (as we read in a sixteenth-
century critic). And Garcilaso about Isabel Freire, and Shakespeare,

the young W. H. Along those lines, biographers have conjectured that the person addressed in Lorca's sonnets was Rafael Rodríguez Rapún or, less convincingly, Juan Ramírez de Lucas. From a literary standpoint, those names have just about the same value as the ones noted above ('Proper names, figured and pretended', wrote a commentator on Quevedo).

As to content – and the same might be said of *Diván del Tamarit* – in the tradition Lorca is embracing, love is dark from birth, the companion of melancholy and of the malady of love which, according to Marsilio Ficino (fifteenth century) afflicts those 'who use love badly and transfer what pertains to contemplation to the concupiscence of touch.' As León Hebreo remembers (sixteenth century), 'true love forces the reason and the person who loves with a marvellous violence in unbelievable ways, and more than any other human hindrance love confuses the mind, where judgement lies; it erases the memory of all other things in order to fill the mind only with itself, and makes him a slave of the beloved.' León Hebreo then reasons that 'unrestraint' is not exclusive to 'wanton love, but pertains to all mighty and great loves, be they honest or dishonest ... Who can deny that honest love may comprise wondrous and boundless desires? What love is nobler than the love of God? Yet what is more ardent and boundless?' And later, Saint John of the Cross tenses his language and generates what the modern gaze can read as utterly erotic – providing a path, certainly, for Lorca who announced in 1928 that *his* poet was no longer the rational, sensual Góngora, and that he was making room for the inspired, the 'evasive' John of the Cross. As he explains in 1930, 'Góngora is the perfect poet of the imagination, verbal equilibrium and the firm line... Saint John of the Cross is just the opposite: flight and longing, yearning for perspective and boundless love.'

Throughout this tradition love is imagined constantly as war and as fire, the sweet bitterness of those martyred by love. In the last analysis, we can speak of erotic desire and its sublimation. Faced with this poetic language and this map (which I have sketched out very roughly), Lorca reads tradition as an experiment and does so, necessarily, through Romanticism, Symbolism, and the avant-garde, all of which by 1935 he has known in their full glory. He also knows the 'convulsive beauty' of surrealism and the equivalence between destruction and love, which his friend Vicente Aleixandre had written about (*Destruction or Love*, 1935). He mines that long tradition for a language of desire – one that cannot be reduced entirely to the utterance of homosexual truth kept silent until then. The poems neither imply that language is the direct, transparent expression of experience, nor are they exercises in literary archaeology.

Thus, the 'Sonnet of the garland of roses' (which has reminded readers of 'Cantico espiritual' by John of the Cross: 'Of flowers and emeralds / plucked in the cool morning / we will make garlands...') accentuates the traditional *carpe diem* motif with a material immediacy, rooted in suffering, that lends it extraordinary urgency ('That garland! Soon! For I am dying! / Weave quickly! sing! moan! sing!') and opposing time and death with total union (concentrated, perhaps, in the paradoxical 'bitten' soul). The same materialist *carpe diem* (we do not find here, as in Quevedo, 'love that is constant after death') reappears in 'The poet tells the truth': 'I want to weep my sorrow and I say this, / so you will love me...' If the poet's desire to be loved is granted, what he begs for is an unending 'skein of I love you, you love me' (and here we *can* remember Quevedo and his definition of love: 'Es un amar solamente ser amado' – love is only being loved), for whatever we leave 'will be for death that does not leave / even a shadow on trembling flesh.' In the 'Sonnet of the sweet complaint' the poet begs not to be abandoned and comes close to the melodramatic and masochistic rhetoric of the bolero ('If you are my cross', 'if I am the dog and you my master'), although he also soars toward rewriting the 'Cántico espiritual': if, in John of the Cross, the Soul in love loses itself voluntarily so that the Husband will find it ('I made myself lost and I was won'), the voice of Lorca's sonnet begs: 'do not let me lose what I have won.'

'Llagas de amor' are 'Wounds of Love'. León Hebreo writes, 'just as an arrow-wound is not healed, even though the bow that sent the arrow be unstrung or broken, so will the wound of true love not be made whole by any joy that fortune may grant or which the beloved may sometime offer, not even by the irremediable loss of the beloved in death.' And John of the Cross, in 'Flame of Living Love': 'Oh, so delicate the wound!' Lorca's first two quatrains enumerate the nuances of that pain, which is a 'garland of love, bed for the wounded, / where sleepless, I dream your presence' (again the 'Cántico espiritual', 'also in the solitude of wounded love'). And no 'prudence' can impede passion (understood as suffering and rapture, in the tradition of the mystical passion of Christ), which one must drink down like a poison.

'The poet asks his love to write him' is an epistolary response with successive intertexts. In the first line, a hyperbole taken from popular speech, 'Amor de mis entrañas' (love of my flesh), recovers its full meaning alongside an antithesis ('living death') that defines love in Petrarch, and in the fourth line comes to be personified in a 'tú' – a you – that is transformed into the entrañas, the very flesh of the lover ('if I live without myself, I want to lose you'). The concept is made from some very well-known lines by Saint Teresa de Jesús: 'I live without living in myself / and hope for such life on high, / that I die because I do not die'. In the second quatrain of Lorca's sonnet the poetic voice tries to construct the world in the absence of the beloved, which is the absence of life. This is not possible. The heart ceases to beat, and moonlight is useless, 'icy honey' that deconstructs Petrarch's and Quevedo's oxymoron (for the latter, love is 'burning ice and icy fire'). The tercets begin with an adversative clause ('But I suffered you...') in defence of the sexual encounter, with vocabulary from the years with Dalí ('I tore my veins') and metonymy habitual in the poet ('as I entwined four nights round / your waist, enemy of the snow') and with two pairs of correlative opposites, 'tiger and dove' and 'bites and lilies', which suggest the impossibility of separating the ferocious physicality of love from spiritual refinement.

'The poet speaks with his love on the telephone.' In *The Guermantes Way* by Proust (published in 1931–32 in the translation of Pedro Salinas and José María Quiroga Pla), the narrator awaits a telephone call from his grandmother, from Paris, with mixed feelings: 'Real presence of this voice so close to me, in its effective separation. But also, anticipations of an eternal separation!' In the sonnet, the voice waters the listener, causing weeping; like the 'bitten soul' mentioned before, the voice spills out and is savoured and penetrates the very marrow of the bones, although it is perceived 'faraway as a dark wounded doe' (reminiscent of the 'wounded stag' of St John of the Cross and of Alberti's song 'My doe, good friend, / my white doe. // The wolves killed it / at the foot of the water').

'The poet asks his love about the "Enchanted City" of Cuenca' is a love letter. The first two quatrains ask about the effects of the fantastic shapes carved by the water in this landscape near the city of Cuenca, among them certain 'walls of pain' seen only by the person writing, with no possible descriptive evocation, and some 'thorns / that crown' that remind us of the Passion of Christ. The first tercet makes the question more intense: 'Did you remember me?' and the second, 'Did you not see my gift? A crown more agreeable than the crown of thorns' – that 'dahlia of sorrows and joys' in contrast to the 'burning heart' of the sender.

But the poem itself – as a letter – is a gift that seeks to fill an absence, as in the 'Sonnet in the manner of Góngora in which the poet sends his beloved a dove'. Sent from Valencia, the dove is the poem and, at the same time, the 'lascivious fledging of the Cyprian goddess' (according to Góngora, remembered by Lorca in his lecture). It has been suggested that that dove relates to the Arab-Andalusian poetry about a pigeon which carries away the heart of the poet. Lorca's dove carries 'a slow flame of love' to the beloved. The second quatrain, intoned to shades of white ('frost, pearl and mist') and the first tercet suggest a phantasmagoric masturbation. The last tercet, in shades of black, takes up the classic motifs of passion and absence: the jailed heart, the prison of love, the dark night, melancholy.

The two quatrains of 'Oh secret voice of dark love!' begin by repeating that complaint before a voice that is a 'wound', a bitter 'needle of gall,' a trampled flower, a defenceless city, a night, a mountain of anguish, a 'pursued voice'; an inner one, fraught with the burning ice that defines love, but inhabiting a place of sterility (as in the sonnet 'Adam', quoted before), which the 'I' wants to distance from himself, in the name of an *other*, non-contradictory love.

'The beloved sleeps on the poet's breast'. He rests there like the soul in 'Dark night' of St John of the Cross: 'On my flowering bosom, / meant only for him, / kept for him alone, / he rested his head to sleep.' But the poet keeps watch and protects the beloved, hiding him from the persecution of a 'law' that oppresses both the flesh and the spirit, imposed perhaps by a 'group of people' who wait menacingly outside (like the Audience in *The Audience*). The poet keeps watch like Christ in the Garden of Olives or a mother singing a lullaby: 'Danger is near. We must grow smaller, very tiny, so that the walls of the little hut won't touch our flesh. They are waiting for us outside' (a lullaby quoted by Lorca in his lecture on Spanish cradle songs).

Lastly, the 'Night of sleepless love' takes place under a full moon, creating a counterpoint between the weeping of the 'I' and his complaints and the disdain and laughter of the 'you' in the first quatrain. In the second – *noche adelante* – the 'you' cries also, but the pain of the 'I' has become agony. Only with dawn do the bodies come together, though they do so through a frozen blood that makes the topos of icy fire more sinister. In the last tercet the 'coral of life' – the rosy fingers of dawn – may be able to reanimate the 'shrouded heart' of the poet.

In a word: tradition in the service of passion.

Translated by Christopher Maurer

Diván del Tamarit

The Tamarit Divan

Gacelas

Del amor imprevisto

Nadie comprendía el perfume
de la oscura magnolia de tu vientre.
Nadie sabía que martirizabas
un colibrí de amor entre los dientes.

Mil caballitos persas se dormían
en la plaza con luna de tu frente,
mientras que yo enlazaba cuatro noches
tu cintura, enemiga de la nieve.

Entre yeso y jazmines, tu mirada
era un pálido ramo de simientes.
Yo busqué, para darte, por mi pecho
las letras de marfil que dicen *siempre*.

Siempre, siempre: jardín de mi agonía,
tu cuerpo fugitivo para siempre,
la sangre de tus venas en mi boca,
tu boca ya sin luz para mi muerte.

Ghazals

Of unforeseen love

No one understood the perfume
of the dark magnolia of your belly.
No one knew that you martyred
a hummingbird of love between your teeth.

A thousand little Persian horses slept
in the moonlit plaza of your forehead
as I entwined four nights round
your waist, enemy of the snow.

Between gypsum and jasmine, your gaze
was a pale branch of seeds.
I searched my breast to give you
the ivory letters that say *always*.

Always, always: garden of my agony,
your body forever fugitive,
the blood of your veins in my mouth,
your mouth with no light for my death.

GACELA II
De la terrible presencia

Yo quiero que el agua se quede sin cauce.
Yo quiero que el viento se quede sin valles.

Quiero que la noche se quede sin ojos
y mi corazón sin la flor del oro;

que los bueyes hablen con las grandes hojas
y que la lombriz se muera de sombra;

que brillen los dientes de la calavera
y los amarillos inunden la seda.

Puedo ver el duelo de la noche herida
luchando enroscada con el mediodía.

Resisto un ocaso de verde veneno
y los arcos rotos donde sufre el tiempo.

Pero no ilumines tu limpio desnudo
como un negro cactus abierto en los juncos.

Déjame en un ansia de oscuros planetas,
pero no me enseñes tu cintura fresca.

Of the terrible presence

I want the water to have no riverbed.
I want the wind to have no valleys.

I want the night to lose its eyes
and my heart its flower of gold;

I want the oxen to speak to the big leaves
and the worm to die of shadow;

let the skull's teeth gleam
and yellows flood the silk.

I can see the wounded night in a duel
struggling, coiled around noon,

I can endure a sunset of green poison
and the broken arches where time suffers.

But do not light up your clean nakedness
like a black cactus open in the reeds.

Leave me longing for dark planets
but do not show me the coolness of your waist.

Del amor desesperado

La noche no quiere venir
para que tú no vengas,
ni yo pueda ir.

Pero yo iré,
aunque un sol de alacranes me coma la sien.

Pero tú vendrás
con la lengua quemada por la lluvia de sal.

El día no quiere venir
para que tú no vengas,
ni yo pueda ir.

Pero yo iré
entregando a los sapos mi mordido clavel.

Pero tú vendrás
por las turbias cloacas de la oscuridad.

Ni la noche ni el día quieren venir
para que por ti muera
y tú mueras por mí.

Of desperate love

Night does not want to come
so you cannot come to me
and I cannot go to you.

But I will go,
even if a sun of scorpions eats my brow.

But you will come,
your tongue burned by a rain of salt.

The day does not want to come
so you will not come
and I cannot go to you.

But I will go
and give my bitten carnation to the toads.

But you will come
through murky sewers of darkness.

Neither night nor day want to come
so that I die for you
and you die for me.

Del amor que no se deja ver

Solamente por oír
la campana de la Vela
te puse una corona de verbena.

Granada era una luna
ahogada entre las yedras.

Solamente por oír
la campana de la Vela
desgarré mi jardín de Cartagena.

Granada era una corza
rosa por las veletas.

Solamente por oír
la campana de la Vela
me abrasaba en tu cuerpo
sin saber de quién era.

Of the love that hides itself

Only to hear
the bell of the Vela
I crowned you with verbena.

Granada was a moon
drowned in ivy.

Only to hear
the bell of the Vela
I tore out my garden of Cartagena.

Granada was a pink doe
among the weathervanes.

Only to hear
the bell of the Vela
I burned in your body
not knowing whose it was.

Del niño muerto

Todas las tardes en Granada,
todas las tardes se muere un niño.
Todas las tardes el agua se sienta
a conversar con sus amigos.

Los muertos llevan alas de musgo.
El viento nublado y el viento limpio
son dos faisanes que vuelan por las torres
y el día es un muchacho herido.

No quedaba en el aire ni una brizna de alondra
cuando yo te encontré por las grutas del vino.
No quedaba en la tierra ni una miga de nube
cuando te ahogabas por el río.

Un gigante de agua cayó sobre los montes
y el valle fue rodando con perros y con lirios.
Tu cuerpo, con la sombra violeta de mis manos,
era, muerto en la orilla, un arcángel de frío.

GHAZAL V

Of the dead child

Every afternoon in Granada,
every afternoon a child dies.
Every afternoon the water
sits down to chat with friends.

The dead wear wings of moss.
The cloudy wind and the clean wind
are two pheasants that fly around the towers
and the day is a wounded boy.

No trace of lark was left in the air
when I found you near the wine caves.
Not a crumb of cloud was left on the earth
when you were drowning by the river.

A water-giant fell on the mountains
and the valley rolled with dogs and irises.
Your body under the violet shadow of my hands
lay dead on the bank, a cold archangel.

De la raíz amarga

Hay una raíz amarga
y un mundo de mil terrazas.

Ni la mano más pequeña
quiebra la puerta del agua.

¿Dónde vas, adónde, dónde?
Hay un cielo de mil ventanas
– batalla de abejas lívidas –
y hay una raíz amarga.

Amarga.

Duele en la planta del pie,
el interior de la cara,
y duele en el tronco fresco
de noche recién cortada.

¡Amor, enemigo mío,
muerde tu raíz amarga!

Of the bitter root

There is a bitter root
and a world of a thousand terraces.

Not even the smallest hand
can break the water-door.

Where are you going, where, where?
There is a sky with a thousand windows –
a battle of livid bees –
and there is a bitter root.

Bitter.

The sole of the foot hurts,
it hurts inside the face
and in the cool trunk
of freshly-cut night.

Love, my enemy,
bite your bitter root!

Del recuerdo de amor

No te lleves tu recuerdo.
Déjalo solo en mi pecho,

temblor de blanco cerezo
en el martirio de enero.

Me separa de los muertos
un muro de malos sueños.

Doy pena de lirio fresco
para un corazón de yeso.

Toda la noche, en el huerto
mis ojos, como dos perros.

Toda la noche, comiendo
los membrillos de veneno.

Algunas veces el viento
es un tulipán de miedo;

es un tulipán enfermo,
la madrugada de invierno.

Un muro de malos sueños
me separa de los muertos.

Of the memory of love

Do not take your memory away.
Leave it in my breast, alone,

a shiver of white cherry tree
in the martyrdom of January.

A wall of bad dreams
separates me from the dead.

I bring you sorrow, a fresh lily
for a heart of plaster.

All night long in the orchard,
my eyes like two dogs.

All night long, eating
quinces of poison.

Sometimes the wind
is a tulip of fear;

a sick tulip,
in the winter dawn.

A wall of bad dreams
separates me from the dead.

La hierba cubre en silencio
el valle gris de tu cuerpo.

Por el arco del encuentro
la cicuta está creciendo.

Pero deja tu recuerdo,
déjalo sólo en mi pecho.

In silence grass covers
the grey valley of your body.

Under the arch of an encounter
hemlock is growing.

But leave your memory with me,
leave it in my breast, alone.

De la muerte oscura

Quiero dormir el sueño de las manzanas,
alejarme del tumulto de los cementerios.
Quiero dormir el sueño de aquel niño
que quería cortarse el corazón en alta mar.

No quiero que me repitan que los muertos no
     pierden la sangre;
que la boca podrida sigue pidiendo agua.
No quiero enterarme de los martirios que da la hierba,
ni de la luna con boca de serpiente
que trabaja antes del amanecer.

Quiero dormir un rato,
un rato, un minuto, un siglo;
pero que todos sepan que no he muerto;
que hay un establo de oro en mis labios;
que soy el pequeño amigo del viento Oeste;
que soy la sombra inmensa de mis lágrimas.

Cúbreme por la aurora con un velo
porque me arrojará puñados de hormigas,
y moja con agua dura mis zapatos
para que resbale la pinza de su alacrán.

Porque quiero dormir el sueño de las manzanas
para aprender un llanto que me limpie de tierra;
porque quiero vivir con aquel niño oscuro
que quería cortarse el corazón en alta mar.

Of the dark death

I want to sleep the sleep of apples,
to be far from the tumult of cemeteries.
I want to sleep the sleep of that child
who wanted to cut his heart out on the high seas.

Do not tell me again that the dead do not bleed
or that the rotting mouth keeps pleading for water.
I don't want to know how grass torments
or how the moon with its snake mouth
works before dawn.

I want to sleep awhile,
a while, a minute, a century;
but let everyone know I have not died,
that there is a stable of gold on my lips,
that I am the West Wind's small friend
and the immense shadow of my tears.

Cover me with a veil at dawn
for dawn will hurl handfuls of ants at me;
and wet my shoes with hard water
so its scorpion-claw may slide off.

Because I want to sleep the sleep of apples
to learn a lament that will cleanse me of earth;
because I want to live with that dark child
who wanted to cut his heart out on the high seas.

Del amor maravilloso

Con todo el yeso
de los malos campos,
eras junco de amor, jazmín mojado.

Con sur y llama
de los malos cielos,
eras rumor de nieve por mi pecho.

Cielos y campos
anudaban cadenas en mis manos.

Campos y cielos
azotaban las llagas de mi cuerpo.

Of marvellous love

With all the gypsum
in bad fields
you were a reed of love, wet jasmine.

With the south wind and flame
in bad skies,
you were a murmur of snow on my breast.

Skies and fields
knotted chains round my hands.

Fields and skies
lashed the wounds of my body.

De la huida

Me he perdido muchas veces por el mar
con el oído lleno de flores recién cortadas,
con la lengua llena de amor y de agonía.
Muchas veces me he perdido por el mar,
como me pierdo en el corazón de algunos niños.

No hay nadie que, al dar un beso,
no sienta la sonrisa de la gente sin rostro,
ni hay nadie que, al tocar un recién nacido,
olvide las inmóviles calaveras de caballo.

Porque las rosas buscan en la frente
un duro paisaje de hueso
y las manos del hombre no tienen más sentido
que imitar a las raíces bajo tierra.

Como me pierdo en el corazón de algunos niños,
me he perdido muchas veces por el mar.
Ignorante del agua, voy buscando
una muerte de luz que me consuma.

Of the flight

I have been lost at sea many times,
my ears full of fresh-cut flowers,
my tongue full of love and agony.
I have been lost at sea many times
as I am lost in the hearts of some children.

No one can give a kiss
without feeling the smile of faceless people,
no one who touches a newborn baby
can forget the immobile skulls of horses.

Because roses search the forehead
for a hard landscape of bone
and human hands can only
imitate roots under the earth.

As I am lost in the hearts of some children
I have been lost at sea many times.
Mindless of the water, I keep searching
for a death of light that consumes me.

Del amor con cien años

Suben por la calle
los cuatro galanes.

Ay, ay, ay, ay.

Por la calle abajo
van los tres galanes.

Ay, ay, ay.

Se ciñen el talle
esos dos galanes.

Ay, ay.

¡Cómo vuelve el rostro
un galán y el aire!

Ay.

Por los arrayanes
se pasea nadie.

Of the hundred year old love

Up the street go
four fine young men.

Ay, ay, ay, ay.

Down the street
go three young men.

Ay, ay, ay.

They bind their waists,
those two young men.

Ay, ay.

How he turns his face –
a young man and the breeze!

Ay.

By the myrtles
no one is walking.

Casidas

Del herido por el agua

Quiero bajar al pozo,
quiero subir los muros de Granada,
para mirar el corazón pasado
por el punzón oscuro de las aguas.

El niño herido gemía
con una corona de escarcha.
Estanques, aljibes y fuentes
levantaban al aire sus espadas.
¡Ay qué furia de amor, qué hiriente filo,
qué nocturno rumor, qué muerte blanca!
¡Qué desiertos de luz iban hundiendo
los arenales de la madrugada!
El niño estaba solo
con la ciudad dormida en la garganta.
Un surtidor que viene de los sueños
lo defiende del hambre de las algas.
El niño y su agonía, frente a frente,
eran dos verdes lluvias enlazadas.
El niño se tendía por la tierra
y su agonía se curvaba.

Quiero bajar al pozo,
quiero morir mi muerte a bocanadas,
quiero llenar mi corazón de musgo,
para ver al herido por el agua.

Qasidas

Of the one wounded by water

I want to go down to the well,
I want to climb the walls of Granada
to see the heart pierced
by the dark awl of the waters.

The wounded boy moaned,
wearing his crown of frost.
Pools, cisterns and fountains
lifted their swords in the air.
Oh, what a fury of love, what a wounding edge,
what nocturnal murmurs, what a white death!
What deserts of light were sinking
the sand-lands of dawn!
The boy was alone,
the city asleep in his throat.
In his dreams a water jet
defends him from the hungry algae.
The boy and his agony, face to face,
were two green rainfalls entwined.
The boy lay down on the earth
and his agony curved.

I want to go down to the well,
I want to die my death in mouthfuls,
I want to fill my heart with moss,
to see the one wounded by water.

Del llanto

He cerrado mi balcón
porque no quiero oír el llanto,
pero por detrás de los grises muros
no se oye otra cosa que el llanto.

Hay muy pocos ángeles que canten,
hay muy pocos perros que ladren,
mil violines caben en la palma de mi mano.

Pero el llanto es un perro inmenso,
el llanto es un ángel inmenso,
el llanto es un violín inmenso,
las lágrimas amordazan al viento,
y no se oye otra cosa que el llanto.

Of the weeping

I have closed my balcony
because I do not want to hear the weeping,
but behind the grey walls
all you can hear is weeping.

There are very few singing angels,
there are very few barking dogs,
a thousand violins fit in the palm of my hand.

But the weeping is an immense dog,
the weeping is an immense angel,
the weeping is an immense violin,
tears muzzle the wind
and all you can hear is the weeping.

De los ramos

Por las arboledas del Tamarit
han venido los perros de plomo
a esperar que se caigan los ramos,
a esperar que se quiebren ellos solos.

El Tamarit tiene un manzano
con una manzana de sollozos.
Un ruiseñor agrupa los suspiros
y un faisán los ahuyenta por el polvo.

Pero los ramos son alegres,
los ramos son como nosotros.
No piensan en la lluvia y se han dormido,
como si fueran árboles, de pronto.

Sentados con el agua en las rodillas
dos valles esperaban al Otoño.
La penumbra con paso de elefante
empujaba las ramas y los troncos.

Por las arboledas del Tamarit
hay muchos niños de velado rostro
a esperar que se caigan mis ramos,
a esperar que se quiebren ellos solos.

Of the branches

Through the groves of Tamarit
the leaden dogs have come,
waiting for the branches to fall,
waiting for them to break on their own.

Tamarit has an apple tree
with an apple of sobs.
A nightingale gathers the sighs
and a pheasant scares them away in the dust.

But the branches are happy,
the branches are like us.
They don't think about the rain, and fall asleep
suddenly, as if they were trees.

Sitting in water up to their knees,
two valleys waited for Autumn.
Dusk with its elephant tread
pushed aside boughs and tree trunks.

In the groves of Tamarit
there are many children with veiled faces
waiting for my branches to fall,
waiting for them to break on their own.

De la mujer tendida

Verte desnuda es recordar la Tierra,
la Tierra lisa, limpia de caballos.
La Tierra sin un junco, forma pura
cerrada al porvenir: confín de plata.

Verte desnuda es comprender el ansia
de la lluvia que busca débil talle,
o la fiebre del mar de inmenso rostro
sin encontrar la luz de su mejilla.

La sangre sonará por las alcobas
y vendrá con espadas fulgurantes,
pero tú no sabrás dónde se ocultan
el corazón de sapo o la violeta.

Tu vientre es una lucha de raíces,
tus labios son un alba sin contorno.
Bajo las rosas tibias de la cama
los muertos gimen esperando turno.

Of the reclining woman

To see you naked is to remember the Earth,
the smooth Earth, clean of horses.
The Earth with no reeds, pure form
closed to the future: silver confine.

To see you naked is to understand the rain
searching for a fragile waist,
or the fever of the sea with its immense face,
never finding the light of its cheek.

Blood will sound in the alcoves
and will come with gleaming swords,
but you will not know where the violet
or the heart of the toad are hiding.

Your belly is a struggle of roots,
your lips are a dawn with no outline.
Under the bed's warm roses
the dead moan, waiting their turn.

Del sueño al aire libre

Flor de jazmín y toro degollado.
Pavimento infinito. Mapa. Sala. Arpa. Alba.
La niña sueña un toro de jazmines
y el toro es un sangriento crepúsculo que brama.

Si el cielo fuera un niño pequeñito,
los jazmines tendrían mitad de noche oscura,
y el toro circo azul sin lidiadores,
y un corazón al pie de una columna.

Pero el cielo es un elefante,
el jazmín es un agua sin sangre,
y la niña es un ramo nocturno
por el inmenso pavimento oscuro.

Entre el jazmín y el toro
o garfios de marfil o gente dormida.
En el jazmín un elefante y nubes
y en el toro el esqueleto de la niña.

Of the dream in open air

Jasmine flower and wounded bull.
Infinite pavement. Map. Room. Harp. Dawn.
The girl dreams of a jasmine bull
and the bull is a bloody sunset that roars.

If the sky were a little child
the jasmine would have half a dark night,
the bull a blue arena with no matadors
and a heart at the base of a column.

But the sky is an elephant,
the jasmine is bloodless water
and the girl a nocturnal branch
on the immense, dark pavement.

Between the jasmine and the bull
are ivory hooks or people asleep.
In the jasmine an elephant and clouds
and in the bull the skeleton of the girl.

De la mano imposible

Yo no quiero más que una mano,
una mano herida, si es posible.
Yo no quiero más que una mano,
aunque pase mil noches sin lecho.

Sería un pálido lirio de cal,
sería una paloma amarrada a mi corazón,
sería el guardían que en la noche de mi tránsito
prohibiera en absoluto la entrada a la luna.

Yo no quiero más que esa mano
para los diarios aceites y la sábana blanca de mi agonía.
Yo no quiero más que esa mano
para tener un ala de mi muerte.

Lo demás todo pasa.
Rubor sin nombre ya. Astro perpetuo.
Lo demás es lo otro; viento triste,
mientras las hojas huyen en bandadas.

QASIDA VI

Of the impossible hand

I want nothing more than a hand,
a wounded hand, if possible.
I want nothing more than a hand
though I have no bed for a thousand nights.

It would be a pale lily of lime,
it would be a dove lashed to my heart,
the guardian who on the night of my transit
absolutely forbids the moon to enter.

I want nothing more than that hand
for the daily oils and the white sheet of my agony.
I want nothing more than that hand
so my death will have a wing.

The rest all passes.
A blush with no name. Perpetual star.
The rest is the other: sad wind,
while the leaves rush away in flocks.

De la rosa

La rosa
no buscaba la aurora:
casi eterna en su ramo,
buscaba otra cosa.

La rosa
no buscaba ni ciencia ni sombra:
confín de carne y sueño,
buscaba otra cosa.

La rosa
no buscaba la rosa:
inmóvil por el cielo,
buscaba otra cosa.

Of the rose

The rose
was not searching for dawn:
almost eternal on its stem,
it was looking for something else.

The rose
did not search for science or shadow:
confine of flesh and dream,
it was looking for something else.

The rose
did not search for the rose:
immobile in the sky,
it was looking for something else.

De la muchacha dorada

La muchacha dorada
se bañaba en el agua
y el agua se doraba.

Las algas y las ramas
en sombra la asombraban,
y el ruiseñor cantaba
por la muchacha blanca.

Vino la noche clara,
turbia de plata mala,
con peladas montañas
bajo la brisa parda.

La muchacha mojada
era blanca en el agua
y el agua, llamarada.

Vino el alba sin mancha,
con cien caras de vaca,
yerta y amortajada
con heladas guirnaldas.

La muchacha de lágrimas
se bañaba entre llamas,
y el ruiseñor lloraba
con las alas quemadas.

La muchacha dorada
era una blanca garza
y el agua la doraba.

Of the golden girl

The golden girl
bathed in the water
and the water turned gold.

In the shade, algae
and branches surprised her
and the nightingale sang
for the white girl.

The clear night came
murky with bad silver,
with bare mountains
under a grey breeze.

The wet girl
was white in the water,
and the water, a flame.

Dawn came with no stain
and a hundred cow faces,
stiff and shrouded
with icy garlands.

The girl of tears
bathed among flames,
and the nightingale wept
with burned wings.

The golden girl
was a white heron
and the water gilded her.

De las palomas oscuras

Por las ramas del laurel
vi dos palomas oscuras.
La una era el sol,
la otra la luna.
Vecinitas, les dije,
¿dónde está mi sepultura?
En mi cola, dijo el sol.
En mi garganta, dijo la luna.
Y yo que estaba caminando
con la tierra por la cintura
vi dos águilas de nieve
y una muchacha desnuda.
La una era la otra
y la muchacha era ninguna.
Aguilitas, les dije,
¿dónde está mi sepultura?
En mi cola, dijo el sol.
En mi garganta, dijo la luna.
Por las ramas del laurel
vi dos palomas desnudas.
La una era la otra
y las dos eran ninguna.

Of the dark doves

In the branches of the laurel
I saw two dark doves.
One was the sun
and the other the moon.
Little neighbours, I said,
where is my tomb?
In my tail, said the sun.
In my throat, said the moon.
As I was walking
with the earth at my waist,
I saw two snow-eagles
and a naked girl.
The one was the other
and the girl was neither.
Little eagles, I said,
where is my tomb?
In my tail, said the sun.
In my throat, said the moon.
In the branches of the laurel
I saw two naked doves.
One was the other
and the two were neither.

Gacela del mercado matutino

Por el arco de Elvira
quiero verte pasar,
para saber tu nombre
y ponerme a llorar.

¿Qué luna gris de las nueve
te desangró la mejilla?
¿Quién recoge tu semilla
de llamarada en la nieve?
¿Qué alfiler de cactus breve
asesina tu cristal?...

Por el arco de Elvira
voy a verte pasar,
para beber tus ojos
y ponerme a llorar.

¿Qué voz para mi castigo
levantas por el mercado!
¿Qué clavel enajenado
en los montones de trigo!
¡Qué lejos estoy contigo,
qué cerca cuando te vas!

Por el arco de Elvira
voy a verte pasar,
para sentir tus muslos
y ponerme a llorar.

Ghazal of the Morning Market

I want to see you pass
through the Arch of Elvira
so I can learn your name
and begin to cry.

What grey nine o'clock moon
has drained the blood from your cheek?
Who gathers your seed
of flame in the snow?
What needle from a brief cactus
murders your crystal?...

I am going to see you walk
through the Arch of Elvira
to drink in your eyes
and begin to cry.

What a voice you raise
to punish me in the marketplace!
What a crazed carnation
among the heaps of wheat!
How far away when I am with you,
how close when you leave!

I am going to see you pass
through the Arch of Elvira,
so I can feel your thighs
and begin to cry.

Sonetos del amor oscuro

Sonnets of Dark Love

Soneto de la guirnalda de rosas

¡Esa guirnalda! ¡pronto! ¡que me muero!
¡Teje deprisa! ¡canta! ¡gime! ¡canta!
que la sombra me enturbia la garganta
y otra vez viene y mil la luz de enero.

Entre lo que me quieres y te quiero,
aire de estrellas y temblor de planta,
espesura de anémonas levanta
con oscuro gemir un año entero.

Goza el fresco paisaje de mi herida,
quiebra juncos y arroyos delicados,
bebe en muslo de miel sangre vertida.

Pero ¡pronto!, que unidos, enlazados,
boca rota de amor y alma mordida,
el tiempo nos encuentre destrozados.

Sonnet of the garland of roses

That garland! Soon! For I am dying!
Weave quickly! sing! moan! sing!
for a shadow clouds my throat
and again the light of January comes a thousand times.

Between your love for me and mine for you,
air of stars and tremor of plant,
a thicket of anemones raises
an entire year with a dark moan.

Delight in the fresh landscape of my wound,
break reeds and delicate streams,
drink blood poured on a thigh of honey.

But hurry! For united, entwined,
mouth broken by love and soul bitten,
time will find us destroyed.

Soneto de la dulce queja

No me dejes perder la maravilla
de tus ojos de estatua, ni el acento
que de noche me pone en la mejilla
la solitaria rosa de tu aliento.

Tengo miedo de ser en esta orilla
tronco sin ramas; y lo que más siento
es no tener la flor, pulpa o arcilla
para el gusano de mi sufrimiento.

Si tú eres el tesoro oculto mío,
si eres mi cruz y mi dolor mojado,
si soy el perro de tu señorío,

no me dejes perder lo que he ganado
y decora las ramas de tu río
con hojas de mi otoño enajenado.

Sonnet of the sweet complaint

Do not let me lose the marvel
of your statue eyes, or the accent
the solitary rose of your breath
places on my cheek at night.

I am afraid to be on this shore –
a trunk with no branches, and what I most regret
is not having the flower, pulp or clay
for the worm of my suffering.

If you are my hidden treasure,
if you are my cross and my wet pain,
if I am the dog and you my master,

do not let me lose what I have won
but adorn the branches of your river
with the leaves of my crazed autumn.

Llagas de amor

Esta luz, este fuego que devora,
este paisaje gris que me rodea,
este dolor por una sola idea,
esta angustia de cielo, mundo y hora,

este llanto de sangre que decora
lira sin pulso ya, lúbrica tea,
este peso del mar que me golpea,
este alacrán que por mi pecho mora,

son guirnalda de amor, cama de herido,
donde sin sueño, sueño tu presencia
entre las ruinas de mi pecho hundido.

Y aunque busco la cumbre de prudencia
me da tu corazón valle tendido
con cicuta y pasión de amarga ciencia.

Wounds of love

This light, this fire that devours,
this grey landscape that surrounds me,
this pain that comes from one idea only,
this anguish of sky, world and hour,

this lament of blood that adorns
a lyre with no pulse, lewd torch,
this weight of the sea that pounds against me,
this scorpion that lives in my breast

are a garland of love, bed for the wounded,
where sleepless, I dream your presence
among the ruins of my sunken breast.

And although I seek the summit of prudence
your heart gives me a valley spread
with hemlock and the passion of bitter knowledge.

El poeta pide a su amor que le escriba

Amor de mis entrañas, viva muerte,
en vano espero tu palabra escrita
y pienso con la flor que se marchita
que si vivo sin mí, quiero perderte.

El aire es inmortal; la piedra inerte
ni conoce la sombra, ni la evita.
Corazón interior no necesita
la miel helada que la luna vierte.

Pero yo te sufrí; rasgué mis venas,
tigre y paloma sobre tu cintura
en duelo de mordiscos y azucenas.

Llena pues de palabras mi locura
o déjame vivir en mi serena
noche del alma para siempre oscura.

The poet asks his love to write to him

Love of my flesh, living death,
in vain I wait for your written word
and think with the withering flower
that if I live without myself, I want to lose you.

The air is immortal; the inert stone
neither knows the shade nor avoids it.
The inner heart does not need
icy honey poured by the moon.

But I suffered you; I tore my veins,
tiger and dove on your waist
in a duel of bites and lilies.

Fill then my madness with words
or let me live in my serene
night of the soul forever dark.

El poeta dice la verdad

Quiero llorar mi pena y te lo digo
para que tú me quieras y me llores
en un anochecer de ruiseñores
con un puñal, con besos y contigo.

Quiero matar al único testigo
para el asesinato de mis flores
y convertir mi llanto y mis sudores
en eterno montón de duro trigo.

Que no se acabe nunca la madeja
del te quiero me quieres, siempre ardida
con decrépito sol y luna vieja,

que lo que no me des y no te pida
será para la muerte que no deja
ni sombra por la carne estremecida.

The poet tells the truth

I want to weep my sorrow and I say this
so you will love me and weep for me
in a dusk of nightingales,
with a dagger, with kisses and with you.

I want to kill the only witness
to the murder of my flowers
and turn my sweat and weeping
into an eternal heap of hard wheat.

Let the skein of I love you, you love me
never end, always burning
under a decrepit sun and an old moon,

for whatever I don't ask and you don't give me
will be for death that does not leave
even a shadow on trembling flesh.

El poeta habla por teléfono con el amor

Tu voz regó la duna de mi pecho
en la dulce cabina de madera.
Por el sur de mis pies fue primavera
y al norte de mi frente flor de helecho.

Pino de luz por el espacio estrecho
cantó sin alborada y sementera
y mi llanto prendió por vez primera
coronas de esperanza por el techo.

Dulce y lejana voz por mí vertida,
dulce y lejana voz por mí gustada,
lejana y dulce voz amortecida,

lejana como oscura corza herida,
dulce como un sollozo en la nevada,
¡lejana y dulce, en tuétano metida!

The poet speaks with his love on the telephone

Your voice watered the dune of my breast
in the sweet wooden booth.
South of my feet it was spring,
and north of my forehead, a fern-flower.

In the narrow space, a pine tree of light
sang with no dawn-music or seed bed,
and my weeping lit for the first time
crowns of hope on the ceiling.

Sweet and faraway voice poured out by me,
sweet and faraway voice tasted by me,
far and sweet faint voice,

faraway as a dark wounded doe,
sweet as a sob in the snowfall,
far and sweet, deep in the marrow.

El poeta pregunta a su amor por la "Ciudad Encantada" de Cuenca

¿Te gustó la ciudad que gota a gota
labró el agua en el centro de los pinos?
¿Viste sueños y rostros y caminos
y muros de dolor que el aire azota?

¿Viste la grieta azul de luna rota
que el Júcar moja de cristal y trinos?
¿Han besado tus dedos los espinos
que coronan de amor piedra remota?

¿Te acordaste de mí cuando subías
al silencio que sufre la serpiente
prisionera de grillos y de umbrías?

¿No viste por el aire transparente
una dalia de penas y alegrías
que te mandó mi corazón caliente?

The poet asks his love about the 'Enchanted City' of Cuenca

Did you like the city the water carved
drop by drop in the centre of the pines?
Did you see dreams and faces and paths
and walls of pain the air lashes?

Did you see the blue crevice of a broken moon
that the Júcar moistens with crystal and trills?
Did your fingers kiss the thorns
that crown the remote stone with love?

Did you remember me when you climbed
to the silence the snake suffers,
prisoner of crickets and shade?

Did you not see in the transparent air
a dahlia of sorrows and joys
that my burning heart sent you?

Soneto gongorino en que el poeta manda a su amor una paloma

Este pichón del Turia que te mando,
de dulces ojos y de blanca pluma,
sobre laurel de Grecia vierte y suma
llama lenta de amor do estoy parando.

Su cándida virtud, su cuello blando,
en lirio doble de caliente espuma
con un temblor de escarcha, perla y bruma
la ausencia de tu boca está marcando.

Pasa la mano sobre su blancura
y verás qué nevada melodía
esparce en copos sobre tu hermosura.

Así mi corazón de noche y día
preso en la cárcel del amor oscura
llora sin verte su melancolía.

Sonnet in the manner of Góngora
in which the poet sends his beloved a dove

This young dove I send you from the Turia,
with sweet eyes and white feathers,
pours over Grecian laurel
a slow flame of love.

Its candid virtue, its soft neck,
in a double lily of hot foam
with a tremor of frost, pearl and mist
is marking the absence of your mouth.

Pass your hand over its whiteness
and you will see what a snowy melody
it scatters in snowflakes over your beauty.

So my heart, night and day
held in the dark prison of love,
not seeing you, weeps its melancholy.

(¡Ay voz secreta del amor oscuro!)

¡Ay voz secreta del amor oscuro!
¡Ay balido sin lanas! ¡Ay herida!
¡Ay aguja de hiel, camelia hundida!
¡Ay corriente sin mar, ciudad sin muro!

¡Ay noche inmensa de perfil seguro,
montaña celestial de angustia erguida!
¡Ay perro en corazón!, voz perseguida,
silencio sin confín, lirio maduro.

Huye de mí, caliente voz de hielo,
no me quieras perder en la maleza
donde sin fruto gimen carne y cielo.

Deja el duro marfil de mi cabeza,
apiádate de mí, ¡rompe mi duelo!,
¡que soy amor, que soy naturaleza!

(Oh secret voice of dark love!)

Oh secret voice of dark love!
Oh bleat without wool! Oh wound!
Oh needle of gall, sunken camellia!
Oh current with no sea, city with no wall!

Oh immense night in steady profile,
celestial mountain, erect anguish!
Oh dog in the heart! pursued voice,
silence with no boundary, ripe lily.

Flee from me, hot voice of ice,
do not try to lose me in the brambles
where fruitlessly flesh and sky moan.

Leave the hard ivory of my head,
have pity on me, break my mourning!
For I am love, I am nature!

El amor duerme en el pecho del poeta

Tú nunca entenderás lo que te quiero,
porque duermes en mí y estás dormido.
Yo te oculto llorando, perseguido
por una voz de penetrante acero.

Norma que agita igual carne y lucero
traspasa ya mi pecho dolorido,
y las turbias palabras han mordido
las alas de tu espíritu severo.

Grupo de gente salta en los jardines
esperando tu cuerpo y mi agonía
en caballos de luz y verdes crines.

Pero sigue durmiendo, vida mía.
¡Oye mi sangre rota en los violines!
¡Mira que nos acechan todavía!

The beloved sleeps on the poet's breast

You will never understand how I love you
because you are asleep and sleep in me.
I hide you, weeping, pursued
by a voice of penetrating steel.

The law that stirs both flesh and star
now pierces my sore breast
and murky words have bitten
the wings of your severe spirit.

In the gardens a group of people leap
on horses of light with green manes.
They wait for your body and my agony.

But go on sleeping, my love.
Listen to my broken blood in the violins!
Look, they are stalking us still!

Noche del amor insomne

Noche arriba los dos, con luna llena,
yo me puse a llorar y tú reías.
Tu desdén era un dios, las quejas mías
momentos y palomas en cadena.

Noche abajo los dos. Cristal de pena
llorabas tú por hondas lejanías.
Mi dolor era un grupo de agonías
sobre tu débil corazón de arena.

La aurora nos unió sobre la cama,
las bocas puestas sobre el chorro helado
de una sangre sin fin que se derrama.

Y el sol entró por el balcón cerrado
y el coral de la vida abrió su rama
sobre mi corazón amortajado.

Night of sleepless love

Night before us and a full moon,
I began to cry and you laughed.
Your disdain was a god, my complaints
a chain of moments and doves.

Night gone, the two of us. Crystal of sorrow,
you were crying for deep distances.
My pain was a group of agonies
on your weak heart of sand.

Dawn drew us together on the bed,
mouths on the icy jet
of endless blood that spills.

And the sun entered the closed balcony
and the coral of life opened its branch
over my shrouded heart.

Notes

The Tamarit Divan

GHAZAL IV
Of the love that hides itself

The poem refers to the bell in the Torre de la Vela, one of the
towers of the Alcazaba in the Alhambra. In the past, the bell
of the Vela chimed at intervals in the night so the farmers in
the Vega would know when to irrigate their fields.

In *Lorca's Late Poetry* Andrew Anderson writes: 'A number
of popular songs, children's games and folk traditions provide
the basis for this poem…' He cites the *tanguillo* and *canción de corro*
referred to below.

Lines 1–2 echo a flamenco *tanguillo*: 'Quiero vivir en Granada /
solamente por oír / la campana de la Vela / cuando me voy
a dormir.' ('I want to live in Granada / only to hear / the bell
of the Vela / when I go to sleep').

Line 8 recalls a children's song which ends '¡ay! ¡ay! ¡ay! / ¿cuándo
vendrá mi amor? / verbena, verbena, / jardín de Cartagena.'
('ay! ay! ay! / when will my love come? / verbena, verbena, /
garden of Cartagena.')

GHAZAL XI
Of the hundred year old love

Line 13: Fragrant, evergreen myrtle bushes abound in the gardens
of Granada and in the Alhambra and the Generalife.

FIRST QASIDA
Of the one wounded by water

> The theme of children drowning also appears in Lorca's poem 'Of the dead child' (GHAZAL V), in 'Little Girl Drowned in the Well' (*Poet in New York*) and in 'Nocturne of the Drowned Youth' (*Six Galician Poems*).

QASIDA III
Of the branches

> See Christopher Maurer's introductory essay 'Violet Shadow' in which he links the image of branches with Lorca's theory of the duende.

QASIDA V
Of the dream in open air

> *Verse 1*: The shape of the map of Spain is often referred to as the *piel de toro* or 'bull's hide'.

Ghazal of the morning market

> Lorca removed the 'Ghazal of the morning market' from his final selection for the *Divan*, but it was posthumously added to the text by his editor in Argentina, Guillermo de Torre.

> The iconic Moorish Arch of Elvira was once the main gate to Granada.

> *Verse 2*: The beloved's gender is implicit in the imagery, as in the poem 'Of the terrible presence' (GHAZAL II).

Sonnets of Dark Love

Sonnet of the garland of roses

This is the only sonnet that was not included among the drafts written on hotel notepaper.

The poet asks his love to write to him

Line 8: Lorca turns the idealised 'honeymoon' (*luna de miel*) into a darker image. The moon in Lorca's poetry is often associated with coldness and death.

Line 14: This line recalls the poem 'Noche oscura' by St John of the Cross, in which the soul goes out in secret to meet God in the darkness.

The poet asks his love about the 'Enchanted City' of Cuenca

The town of Cuenca is built on a rocky cliff overlooking the Júcar river. In verse 3 Lorca evokes the sinuous path bordered by trees and bushes that climbs from the river to the city.

Sonnet in the manner of Góngora in which the poet sends his beloved a dove

The title refers to the poet Góngora (1561–1627) from Córdoba. In Lorca's lecture 'The poetic image of Don Luis de Góngora', he praises Góngora's innovative and sensuous use of metaphor and the way he harmonises contrasting images.

The beloved sleeps on the poet's breast

Line 2: 'porque duermes en mí y estás dormido'. The word 'dormido' is the only explicit reference in these sonnets to the lover's gender.

Lines 2 and 9–11 suggest the agony of Christ in Gethsemane where his disciples slept while he prayed, and where Judas led 'a great multitude with swords and staves' (Mark 14:43) to him.

Notes on the contributors

Jane Duran was born in Cuba, the daughter of a Spanish exile
and an American mother. She was brought up in the United States
and Chile, and lives in London. Her collection of poems, *Breathe
Now, Breathe* (Enitharmon Press, 1995) won the Forward Prize
for Best First Collection. Subsequently Enitharmon published
Silences from the Spanish Civil War (2002), *Coastal* (2005), *Graceline* (2010)
and *American Sampler* (2014). Together with Gloria García Lorca
she translated Lorca's *Gypsy Ballads* (Enitharmon Press, 2011).
She received a Cholmondeley Award in 2005.

Gloria García Lorca was born in NYC during her parents' exile from
Spain. She is the daughter of the poet's younger brother Francisco,
and Laura de los Ríos. Gloria García Lorca received her Bachelor
of Arts degree from Sarah Lawrence College, NY and then moved
to Madrid where she has lived ever since. She has translated
Jane Duran's book *Silences from the Spanish Civil War* into Spanish, and
with Duran she translated the *Gypsy Ballads*. Gloria García Lorca
is a ceramist, painter and sculptor. Her work has been exhibited
in Europe and the United States.

Christopher Maurer, Professor of Spanish at Boston University, is the co-editor of Lorca's complete letters, *Epistolario completo* (Cátedra) and editor of his *Collected Poems* (New York: Farrar, Straus and Giroux, 2002). He is the author of an award-winning biography of the American painter Walter Inglis Anderson; a book with María Estrella Iglesias about a Southern family of artists and potters (*Dreaming in Clay on the Coast of Mississippi*); and a book of essays about the elements of poetic creation, *The Complete Perfectionist: A Poetics of Work* (Swan Isle Press), based on aphorisms by Juan Ramón Jiménez. In 2013 he co-curated with Andrés Soria Olmedo an important exhibition on Lorca's *Poet in New York* at the New York Public Library.

Andrés Soria Olmedo is Professor of Spanish Literature at the University of Granada and a Fellow of the Reale Collegio di Spagna in Bologna. He has also been a Visiting Scholar at Harvard University (1987) and Visiting Professor at UCLA (1996, 2002), New York University (2006) and Brown University (2011). His research mainly focuses on Spanish literature of the renaissance and the twentieth century, in particular 'The Generation of '27'. He has edited Pedro Salinas/Jorge Guillén *Correspondencia* (1923–1951), published by Tusquets in 1992, and his book *Fábula de Fuentes: tradición y vida literaria en Federico García Lorca* was published by Publicaciones de la Residencia de Estudiantes in 2004. He has co-curated, with Christopher Maurer, the exhibition *Back Tomorrow: Federico García Lorca / Poet in New York*, at the New York Public Library (2013).

First published in 2017
by Enitharmon Press
www.enitharmon.co.uk

Reprinted May 2019

Distributed in the UK by
Central Books
Freshwater Road
Dagenham RM8 1RX

Distributed in the USA and Canada
by Independent Publishers Group
814 North Franklin Street
Chicago, IL 60610, USA
www.ipgbooks.com

ISBN 978-1-910392-14-0

British Library Cataloguing-in-Publication Data.
A catalogue record for this book is available from the British Library.

Designed in 2016 by John Morgan studio
Reprinted in England by Short Run Press

ENITHARMON PRESS